ALL★STAR ANIMALS

Pets who'd rather play than stay

Brutus, a miniature dachshund, goes skydiving with his owner, Ron Sirull, of Phoenix, Arizona.

PHOTOGRAPH BY TOM SANDERS/AERIAL FOCUS

Charlie, a 19-year-old chimpanzee, is a black belt in American karate. To find out more about him, turn to page 24.

PHOTOGRAPH BY SAM BARCROFT

Contents

Nutty Profession

Twiggy is a world-famous water skier who performs on the international boat show circuit. The one-pound, bushy-tailed star is towed behind a remote-control boat that travels at speeds up to five miles per hour in a 25-foot pool. Twiggy clutches the line, stands on custom-made miniature skis, and rips waves made from the boat's wake. She is the fifth gray squirrel that Lou Ann Best of Sanford, Florida, has trained to master water skiing.

PHOTOGRAPH BY STEPHEN HOLMAN/AP

Did you know...

Pigs don't sweat. They roll in the mud in warm weather because the mud keeps them cool.

Road Hogs

Racing Pigs

One of the most popular attractions at state and county fairs is pig racing. A day at the races normally features four porkers with silly names, such as Forrest Rump, Britney Spareribs, Arnold Schwarzenhogger, and Swinefeld. The pigs scamper around an 80- to 190-foot circular track in a race that lasts less than a minute. What does the speediest swine win for busting his chops? Oreo cookies. The losers get the crumbs.

It's Good!

Shamu the whale

Shamu has a whale of a time wowing crowds at Sea World, in San Diego, California. On January 20, 2003, one week before the Tampa Bay Buccaneers and Oakland Raiders came to town for Super Bowl XXXVII, Shamu performed a gravity-defying stunt. The 12-ton killer whale rocketed out of the pool and nailed a tail-flip. Shamu flipped her tail flukes forward as a trainer tossed her a giant inflatable football. Using her tail, she then kicked the ball through a foam goalpost.

Did you know ...

The Orca, or killer whale, is the largest member of the dolphin family.

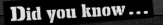

PHOTOGRAPH BY BOB COUEY/AP

Surf's Up

Buddy, the surfing dog

Some dogs chase cats. Buddy chases waves at the beaches in Ventura, California. The 5-year-old Jack Russell terrier can balance his weight on a foam bodyboard because he practices six hours a day. His owner, Bruce Hooker, takes Buddy and his board into the water and then releases them to the waves. Hooker doesn't stand next to Buddy as he rides the waves — he leaves the dog to hang ten. Buddy started out surfing in shallow water but now goes out farther into the ocean to catch bigger waves. But he always wears a life vest, in case of a wipeout.

Did you know ...

The Jack Russell terrier is a popular breed in Hollywood. Jack Russells have appeared on hit TV shows such as *Frasier* and *Wishbone*.

ALL-STAR ANIMALS

11

Did you know...

Dogs can be trained to become excellent swimmers. The dog paddle is a basic stroke taught to beginning human swimmers.

NEPTUNE

SNORKEL INN
DIVE SHOP

Scuba, Scuba Doo

Hooch, the scuba-diving dog

Meet Hooch, the scuba-diving pooch. She wears a specially designed $1,200 wet suit and a fishbowl-like helmet that's attached to an air tank with a breathing tube. Hooch, a mix of Australian cattle dog and King Charles spaniel, stays underwater for about 15 minutes during each dive. She has made at least 14 dives with her owner, Sean Herbert.

Dog on Board

Tyson, the skateboarding dog

Jim Blauvelt had to paws — uh, pause — when he saw his bulldog, Tyson, rolling solo on a skateboard in their backyard, in Huntington Beach, California. Tyson was just a 1-year-old pup when he taught himself to ride on a board. He's been rolling for more than two years. The 65-pound English Bulldog starts out with his right paws on the 39" skateboard and his left paws running beside it. Once he builds up speed, he puts all four paws on the skate deck. He can ride for up to two miles.

Did you know . . .

The first doggie skydive was performed by Katie, a British Jack Russell terrier, in 1987. She jumped 3,658 meters (12,000 feet), the record at the time.

Rope Tricks

Olive Oyl, the jump-roping dog

Maybe Olive Oyl's owners should change her name to Skippy. On July 8, 1998, the Russian wolfhound set a world doggie jump-roping record, in Los Angeles, California. She skipped the most revolutions of a jump rope by a dog in one minute (63).

TOM SANDERS/AERIAL FOCUS

Air Time

Brutus, the sky-diving dog

Ron Sirull, of Phoenix, Arizona, knew that his dog loved to feel the wind as he stuck his nose out a car window. So Sirull, a skydiver, thought that Brutus, a miniature dachshund, might like to try his sport. From 1993 to 1998, Brutus made more than 100 parachute jumps strapped to his owner's chest. Sirull said

Brutus would get excited the minute he saw his gear. Brutus's vet and the Arizona Humane Society said that jumping was safe for the pooch. Brutus set the world canine record for highest jump, 4,572 meters (15,000 feet), on May 20, 1997, above Lake Elsinore, in California. Brutus died in 1998 of natural causes. Now, Sirull jumps with another miniature dachshund, also named Brutus.

Hangin'

Buddy, the hang-gliding dog

Buddy, a 10-year-old yellow Labrador, has been hang-gliding since 1994, when he was a 6-month-old puppy. He and his owner, Bill Kimball of Spring Valley, California, have taken more than 100 flights. Kimball, a 30-year hang-gliding veteran, avoids doing loops or tricky maneuvers with Buddy onboard because the dog is heavy (about 85 pounds). Buddy is strapped to the glider in a special harness with holes for his legs. He sometimes barks at seagulls and pelicans on his flights — but mostly, he just enjoys the view from above.

Hot Dogs

Stars of the ESPN Great Outdoor Games

These canine athletes are triple threats. They competed in hunting, jumping, and running at the 2004 ESPN Great Outdoor Games. Ransom *(bottom)*, a border collie, zipped through obstacle courses to win the "Large Dog Agility" and "Agility Superweave" events. Hamlet *(below, right)*, a Jack Russell terrier, jumped through hoops to win the "Small Dog Agility" title. Little Morgan *(top right)*, a black Labrador, leaped the farthest distance off a dock (23' 1") to earn the second "Big Air" gold medal of his career. He set the world record for longest jump (26' 6") in 2002.

8 9 10 11 12 13 14 15 16

ALL-STAR ANIMALS

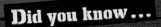

Did you know...

The rare owl parrot, found in New Zealand, has an owl-like face and green feathers. It cannot fly.

Watch the Birdie

Squawk the parrot

Squawk is the Tony Hawk of birds. The 13-year-old parrot has been skateboarding for six years. She pushes an eight-inch-long skateboard along flat surfaces and ramps. Squawk is no chicken on a bicycle or roller skates, either. She pedals a mini-bike equipped with training wheels and wears custom-made skates that she slides with her claws. Squawk talks and can perform more than 150 tricks, including whistling "Pop Goes the Weasel."

PHOTOGRAPHS BY TANI ROBAR

Did you know . . .

A rat can swim for three days straight before it gets exhausted and drowns.

The Xtreme Rat Challenge has been held each year since 1974 at Nebraska Wesleyan University, in Lincoln, Nebraska. A group of students train white lab rats to compete in hurdles, long jumping, rope climbing, tightrope walking, and weightlifting. Mini-medals are awarded to the winning rodents.

Xtreme Challenge Rats

Rodent Rivals

ALL-STAR ANIMALS

'Trunk Dunkin'

Gunther, the basketball-playing elephant

Here's an elephant that's tons of fun — all 2,470 pounds of him. Gunther is an Asian elephant in the Ringling Brothers and Barnum & Bailey Circus. His specialty is shooting hoops. He takes high-percentage shots. He holds a basketball in his trunk, rises on his hind legs, and slam-dunks the ball into an eight-foot-high basket.

Did you know ...

An elephant uses its trunk as a hand. The trunk can hold an object as big as a 600-pound log or as small as a coin.

PHOTOGRAPH COURTESY OF FELD ENTERTAINMENT

Did you know...

The average Asian elephant is 9' tall. The first known elephant on earth was called Moeritherium. It stood about 2' tall and had no trunk.

Ride On

Shirley, the tricycle-riding elephant

Nine-year-old Shirley the Elephant got lots of laughs when she rode her tricycle as part of the Ringling Brothers and Barnum & Bailey Circus. The 7,000-pound Asian elephant pedaled a 700-pound pink trike made of steel. She could ride as far as 100 feet. Her trainer, Patrick Harned, says the pedaling motion is similar to the movements elephants make in the wild when they roll logs with their feet.

Shirley now lives at the Ringling Brothers and Barnum & Bailey Center for Elephant Conservation, in Polk County, Florida.

PHOTOGRAPH COURTESY OF FELD ENTERTAINMENT

Did you know...

Elephants have a keen sense of hearing. They can make and hear sounds below the range of human hearing. These low sounds travel far. Elephants can communicate with each other from as far away as six miles.

PHOTOGRAPH BY SUKREE SUKPLANG/REUTERS

Scoring Stampede

Soccer-playing elephants

The 2004 European Soccer Championship was held in Portugal. But it generated plenty of excitement half a world away, in Ayutthaya, Thailand. A group of men there celebrated the tournament by holding their own match — with a twist. Men on foot played soccer against elephants with male riders. The elephants had the flags of the participating European teams painted on their sides. The match ended in a 5–5 tie. No word on a rematch.

Kickin' It

Charlie the chimpanzee is a certified black belt in American karate. The 4' 8", 200-pound chimp earned the honor in 1998 by performing a required series of kicks and strikes. One of Charlie's most impressive moves is a jump-spinning heel kick. He jumps straight up in the air, makes a 360-degree spin, and kicks with his foot. Charlie began learning martial arts when he was 2 years old by aping his owner and karate instructor, Carmen Presti of Niagara Falls, New York.

PHOTOGRAPH BY SAM BARCROFT

Did you know...

The chimpanzee is one of the most intelligent animals. Chimps can reason, make decisions, and express emotions such as joy or sadness.

ade

Primate on Ice

Bernie, the hockey-playing chimp

Bernie was one of the stars of *MVP: Most Valuable Primate,* in 2000. He, along with two other chimps, played Jack, a smart chimp who joins a struggling hockey team. To prepare for the role, Bernie was outfitted in custom-made hockey gear and taught to skate and shoot slap shots. You may have seen Bernie skating between periods at NHL games to promote the film. He also appeared in NHL exhibition games.

Did you know . . .

Chimpanzees are one of four kinds of apes. The others are gibbons, gorillas, and orangutans.

Did you know . . .

You can spot Capuchin monkeys by the dark circular patch of fur on the tops of their heads. Capuchins can live as long as 40 years.

Ben, a 60-pound border collie, rounds up sheep at rodeos. But it's the monkey on his back that gets the crowds going wild. Whiplash, a seven-pound Capuchin monkey, rides atop Ben in a saddle and wears a cowboy hat, bandanna, western shirt, and chaps. He and Ben are owned by Tom Lucia, a veteran rodeo performer. Using a whistle, Lucia commands Ben to run around in the arena as Whiplash swings his saddle from side to side and yelps at the audience. Whiplash, age 18, has been riding for 15½ years. He and Ben perform about 200 shows a year.

PHOTOGRAPH BY PATRICK PRICE/REUTERS

Monkey Business

Whiplash, the cowboy monkey

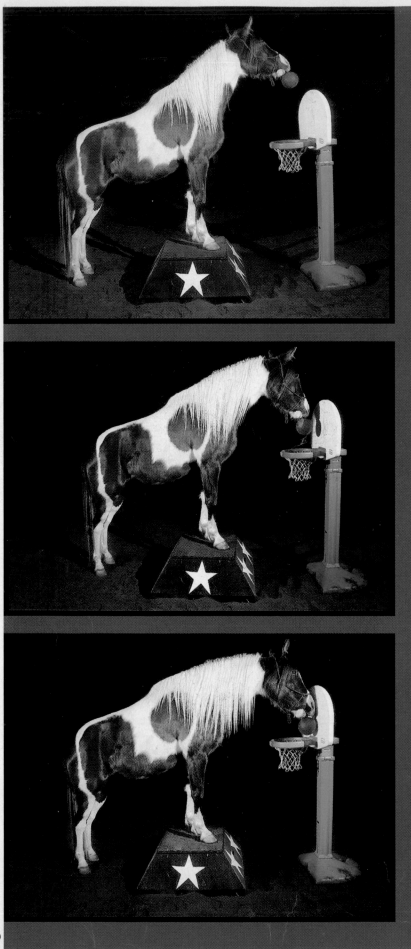

If a basketball player can play H-O-R-S-E, why can't a horse play basketball? Dazzle, a half-Arabian pinto from Lithopolis, Ohio, can — and does. The 4-year-old started playing hoops at about six months old with his owner, LaDora Flood. Dazzle uses a ball with a small handle, which he grips between his teeth. He runs at full speed and slams the ball into the hoop. Or he trots up to the basket, plants his front hooves on a small platform, and dunks. Dazzle likes to rack up the points — he gets a cookie for each basket he makes.

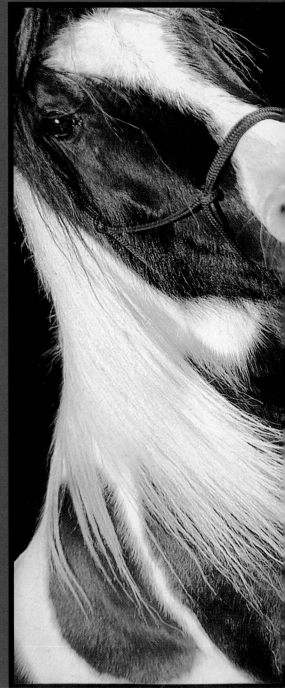

Slammin' and Jammin'

Dazzle, the basketball-playing horse

ALL-STAR ANIMALS

PHOTOGRAPHS BY ROBERT CAPLIN

Home Stretch

★ Squirrel in training

This furry little fellow scampered onto the track during the last lap of the girls' 800-meter race at the 2003 CYO Area E Track and Field Championships, in Upper Dublin, Pennsylvania. Could he be training to become the next Twiggy?

PHOTOGRAPH BY ROBERT LONGHITANO